New Jersey Tenants' Rights

By Angela Davis

Dedicated to:

My children Ajani, Zuri and Judah. You stood with me no matter how fierce the battles. Your love, prayers and support made all the difference in the world.

Table of Contents

I have good news and bad news for New Jersey tenants. The good news is that we have arguably the best and strongest laws to protect tenants in the country. The bad news is many landlords are ignoring them… at your expense.

I believe that the vast majority of landlords in this country are good, honest and hard working people. However, as in any business, there are some who will engage in unethical if not outright illegal and unjust practices. Stories of the heartlessness of these landlords and the tactics they use have become increasingly bold. There was one case in which a young couple with a 3 year old daughter had their landlord take their payment only to have that same landlord attempt to evict them illegally by having the sheriff accompany him as he changed the locks. Thankfully, the young mother had not been feeling well and had taken a day off from work. When she heard someone jiggling the door handle she ran down the steps and because she knew her rights she was able to stop this illegal lockout. This happened not once but twice.

I also have had the unfortunate experience of having a Warrant of Removal tacked to my door even though I owed no money. Thinking it was an innocent mistake I brought it to the attention of the property manager. After initially lying and saying that the money hadn't been paid on time, she then said that they had rescinded the Warrant of Removal. Because I didn't trust her I called courthouse only to find that she had lied about rescinding the warrant as well. This attempted eviction was also stopped because I knew my rights.

I can't emphasize enough just how important it is for tenants to know their rights. Anyone could do anything they want to do if we don't arm ourselves with some very basic information. Surprisingly, in my case, management still attempted to bypass laws and statutes even though they knew I had some awareness of the law. No one will truly know just how many families have been displaced because of the practices of landlords who fail to follow laws as set for in the New Jersey Anti-Eviction Act. With this book I seek to share what I have come to learn about our rights. I am not a lawyer. I am, however, a social worker and community activist who believes in social justice.

You can't fight what you don't know; failure to make repairs, illegal lock outs, failure to respond to complaints of noisy neighbors, evictions based on false information, attempts to make you pay for services you are not responsible for. All of these are on the rise as apartments in New Jersey become more scarce. Some unethical landlords have become emboldened in their dubious practices because they know that another prospective tenants are in abundance and that rental properties are in high demand.

In the wake of the recession, across the country many state and local budgets have been cut dramatically. Of course it goes without saying that many small, struggling non profits that help the working class and poor would also be affected. Many of these agencies who rely on government funds as well as private contributions have seen their budgets plummet as well. Cutting staff and services was a necessary step to ensure that their program survives and stays true to it's mission. Among the many programs affected is South Jersey Legal Services.

The State of the Nation's Housing Report comes out annually and looks at trends in the housing market. According to the 2014 report, households who rent grew by more than half a million people in 2013. This makes it the highest it's been in decades http://www.huffingtonpost.com/courtney-craig/study-renting-is-hot-but-_b_5536935.html . When you consider that many people lost homes as a result of the housing crisis you can understand why there are so many new renters vying for a limited number of rentals.

New Jersey just happens to lead the nation in protection of tenants' rights. This is due in large part to the efforts of New Jersey Tenants Organization (NJTO) http://www.njto.org/ and the fight that they began back in 1969. It was they who laid the ground work for many of the laws that groups like Legal Services of New Jersey and it's satellite office South Jersey Legal Services (commonly referred to as Legal Aid in the Camden area) seek to enforce.

Often, landlords have expensive lawyers, lobbyists and other high paid professionals looking out for their best interest. In fact, many of the non profits fighting for our rights will tell you that they spend the majority of their time defending rights that have already been won. Tenants who are trying to keep a safe and decent roof over their family's head is left with no option but to become educated about what their rights are. A lot of nonsense perpetrated by unscrupulous property owners and managers would be scaled back a great deal when tenants become knowledgeable. The Bible states, *"My people are destroyed for a lack of knowledge..."* Hosea 4:6. These words are ringing true for renters in New Jersey and all over the country.

Because there are people who are far more qualified than I am to cite and interpret the law for you I will not be doing so. More importantly, I am not a lawyer. I don't work for a law firm and this book does not provide any legal advice.

I am a social worker who has spent more than 20 years linking people with resources to assist them in making the best decision for their situation. This book is no different. I am simply providing actual cases and relaying the actions taken and citing resources tenants used to achieve a favorable outcome. I highly recommend that anyone who can afford a lawyer should hire one if one is needed. If you can't afford one then contact your local Legal Services of New Jersey Office or a Pro Bono program. Wherever you choose to go for legal help, please make sure that the person actually is experienced in landlord-tenant law. Not to do so could end up costing you precious time, money and energy.

This endeavor to educate NJ tenants came about as a result of my own experience with an apartment complex that I had resided in for several years. I'm not writing based on philosophy and theories. I'm writing based on real life experiences of myself and other tenants.

Things were generally good until a new apartment manager was hired. She had originally been hired as our secretary but when yet another manager left (we'd had 5 in the 3 years since this owner took over). One of the first things the new owner did was to send everybody an application packet. I told people not to fill it out because there was no way that we needed to apply for apartments we already lived in. When a new owner takes over a complex they inherit the tenants that are already there the same as they inherited anything associated with the apartment, good or bad.

Another development was that a lot of tenants had made payment arrangements with the previous owners were told by the new owner that there was no record of their payment. People were devastated. These tenants had violated **Rule #1**: **Always Get A Receipt!** Because the previous owner had been kind enough to put people on a payment plan tenants became relaxed and trusted management to the point that they didn't challenge the fact that the manager did not give them a receipt. If nothing else, you must always, always, always get a receipt!

Back to this new secretary/property manager. It actually did occur to some us that this individual went from being a secretary to a property manager in the space of 24 hours. In New Jersey, a person has to be licensed by the Real Estate Commission to manage a property…EXCEPT…if they are working directly for the owner. This was the case with the new manager, Andrea. As a secretary, she had been so nice, pleasant and always smiling at any and everyone who came into the office. By day 7 of her new position, all of that had changed.

I came into the office to explain what I thought was a mistake that her new assistant had made. I'd made payment arrangements and submitted money that they had accepted. A couple of days later I received a notice that I hadn't contacted the office to make payment arrangements so I was being referred to their attorney. When I began telling Andrea that a payment had been made and that her secretary was in error she suddenly became rude and hostile. Then out of nowhere she said, " look…the owners don't care how cute your kids are they want their money!" The only thing I could do was sit there with my mouth open and look confused. I was trying to figure how exactly the mention of my kids would need to be a part of this conversation.

We finally sorted through the paperwork and straightened everything out. As I was walking out the door she began waving a stack of papers as she hollers behind me, " do you think I enjoy referring all of these people to our attorney?" I'm thinking she probably did…and…I could've sworn there was a faint smile on her face.

Rule #2: Read Everything

Wouldn't you know it, I fell behind on my payment a couple of weeks after Andrea's promotion. At the time, money was tight. The terms of the tenants' payment agreement had changed making the payments due much sooner and with a larger 'good faith' deposit. I don't blame management at all because the rules had been very lax prior to this. Renting properties is a business, after all, and the payment agreements had been extended as a courtesy.

As expected, I received a notice of eviction. At the time I was 3 weeks late. I was not eligible to receive any housing assistance because I was not receiving cash from TANF. I immediately went to Camden County Board of Social Services and applied for cash then I applied for an emergency voucher and promptly received it to pay the unpaid portion of my rent. Not long after, I closed my TANF case as it was no longer necessary and I had also started an herbal business.

To receive a rental voucher you must be able to explain why you were unable to pay your rent. You should keep all receipts because the providing agency will ask you for them as proof as to how you spent your money. Emergency Assistance also insists on seeing a Certificate of Occupancy. That's the sticker on the window which indicates that your unit has passed inspection and is safe to live in. When I told Andrea I needed this in order to get the voucher she said she couldn't find it. In NJ a landlord can't file for eviction unless there is a Certificate of Occupancy (http://www.lsnjlaw.org/Housing/Landlord-Tenant/Evictions/Pages/Defenses-to-Eviction.aspx#.VNDmhCxkDGs) . Andrea had to sign the voucher and agree to drop all eviction proceedings against me upon receiving the voucher. Everything was paid. No eviction was ordered. Life was good....

… until the end of June when my daughter noticed a paper on our door. It was a Warrant of Removal from the court. It said that we had to be out in 3 business days. I wasn't terribly upset because I was sure it was an oversight on Andrea's part. After all, I had documentation everywhere showing the rent had been paid. I emailed her, as well as her supervisor and Regional Manager, Carol. I read through the document just the same. It said that if I felt that the Warrant of Removal should not be granted I needed to answer this in writing and submit a copy to the court and landlord. Again, I was sure it was a mistake but I wrote a statement anyway. Better safe than sorry.

When I hadn't gotten any response I went to the office to let Andrea know she had made a mistake. I almost fell out when she refused to admit the 'mistake' and then proceeded to tell me that both I and Emergency Assistance had paid late. I calmly asked her if she was going to stick with that story. I then used video on my cell phone to record the fact that I had served her notice of my answer to the Warrant of Removal. She then stated repeatedly, "I'm going to rescind the Warrant of Removal." She even sent me an email stating as much (of which I have a copy).

Because I didn't trust her I called the courthouse and, of course, she had not rescinded the Warrant of Removal. I provided proof of payment to the court and was granted a **Hearing To Show Cause. This would be the paperwork that you would file in response to the landlord's motion against you. In it I had to explain to the judge why the Warrant of Removal should not be enforced.** I was given paperwork and instructed by the court clerk to provide the complex with information for the hearing. Again, I videotaped myself giving notice to the complex, this time to Andrea's assistant, Makini, who begins to tell me that it was all the fault of the corporate office. She goes on to say that no one from the office would be there because everyone would be attending the new Tenant's Appreciation Day celebration that the complex was having. I couldn't believe my ears. She was actually trying to get me not to go to court! Meanwhile, I'm thinking to myself, *"what tenants would really appreciate is not having their payments disappear into thin air and being hauled into court for an unjustified eviction."* I calmly informed her that I would be unable to attend as I would be in court telling the judge my story.

I was able to get this all on my cell phone video. I personally feel that a cell phone video acts as a poor man's lawyer. When there's a video recorder people treat you with a certain level of respect that they wouldn't before. When there's a video recorder people choose their words much more carefully. When there's video recorder people who may not have the best intentions seem to get nervous. They may refuse to speak at all in the presence of the video recorder because they know that their own words could be used against them. Not everyone who refuses to speak on camera has something to hide but I think it's safe to say that those who have something to hide, usually don't want to speak on camera.

Finally, our court date arrives. Their attorney asks to speak to me in the hallway. I tell her that all the money has been paid. She says she knows but there was still the matter of July's rent. I informed her that I had July's but I would not be paying the late fee because the only reason I was late was because the complex had made my payment disappear and I was unwilling to pay one more cent without the court's involvement.

The hearing went well. The judge saw that all monies had been paid. He demanded to know why we were here since everything was paid. I thought that this was a brilliant question. I looked at the complex' attorney. She said, " well your Honor, there is the matter of July's rent." I held up the money for July's rent. The eviction was dismissed.

Rule #3...If you don't like what the opposing attorney is saying or the mediator, you always have the right to reject their terms and tell your story to the judge. It is common for both sides of a case to try and work things out either by negotiating directly with each other or with their attorney. Mediation is also used. This is when a third person, who has no ties to the case, acts as a mediator (middleman) to help both parties come to an agreement. Whichever method you use to try and resolve the dispute...**get it in writing!** Document everything that is agreed on and both parties should have a copy. These agreements can be referenced in court.

If I had failed to do any number of things my kids and I would have been out on the street. First and foremost, we had all of our receipts and proof of payment. We had a copy of the letter from Emergency Assistance that clearly showed that not only had payment been made, it had been made on time. We had proof of when the money orders had been cashed. We read through the paperwork that the sheriff had taped to our door. No matter how upsetting the sight of a legal notice may be, you absolutely have to read through it or have someone else read through it for you. It usually tells you what you need to do to not have the adverse action take place.

Two weeks after our Show Cause Hearing on July 25th, I submitted 2 maintenance requests. The first request asked that a gap between my bedroom wall and the floorboard be fixed. The second request asked that they fix the concrete wall that adjoined my upstairs neighbor's. It was crumbling at the base and I felt that it may compromise the integrity of the entire structure. A gentleman whom I had never met before introduced himself as the new maintenance man. He told me that there was no danger of the wall collapsing and that the wall's loose brick was simply a cosmetic issue and they would take care of it as soon as they were able.

By August 8th I still had not heard back from Summit and of course no work had been done. I called Lindenwold Township and informed them that Summit still had not filled the space between my bedroom wall and the floorboard. I explained that there is a huge gap that allows any critter from outside to come in, including beetles and snails.

At 1:54pm a gentleman, whom I assumed to be from inspections, called me back. I relayed the same information to him. He told me he would call Summit's Office "to find out what's going on." I was unaware that inspections were done via telephone. I had never heard of anything like this. After not hearing back from him I called him again and left a message inquiring as to the outcome. By 3:55pm, just two hours later, Leasing Assistant, Makini Corsey came over and gave me a paper which stated that the following day my apartment would be inspected for bedbugs based on information given to them by Inspector Jim Hawthorn from Lindenwold Borough Code Enforcement. Makini went on to say that Mr. Hawthorn's report stated that I complained of having bedbugs. She gave me a notice that stated that an inspector and a technician from Erlich Pest Control would come to inspect my apartment the following day.

You'll notice that the report states that I never mentioned having bedbugs to them. That was absolutely true, the reason being, that I never had a bedbug problem...ever! By the way, since when do bedbugs need a gap in the wall to get into adjoining apartments? Bedbugs need only the smallest little cracks and crevices to move from unit to unit. Bedbugs crawling through the gap in the wall was the least of my worries.

Keep in mind that at that time that I received this notice, it was practice in New Jersey for landlords to pay for extermination of bedbugs unless the tenant states that the infestation originated in their unit. Furthermore, it was stated right in my lease that management would pay for bedbug extermination services. At the time that she brought the notice over, however, I didn't know this. I was under the false impression that tenants were responsible for the bill that could easily run into the hundreds of dollars. It wasn't until I started researching our rights that I learned who was responsible for what and when.

I videotaped her statement. I informed her that I don't have a bedbug problem nor have I ever had a bedbug problem and had never seen one. In fact, I sell Diatomaceous Earth to people in the community so they can eradicate bug problems without resorting to toxic chemicals. Enough children have to deal with the lingering effects of poisonous pesticides being sprayed in and around their homes.

Diatomaceous Earth works so well that we haven't needed an exterminator since 2010 when we first started using it. Months later, 2 people who were in a position to know told me that an adjoining unit had previously been treated for bedbugs. They both mentioned the same unit on separate occasions.

It's my opinion that management had this knowledge and surmised that I also would have the same problem as the adjoining apartment. This would certainly have been the case had it not been for the Diatomaceous Earth. It had even gotten rid of those problem beetles that I had initially complained about. My family and I have no pest problems, thanks be to God. No roaches, bedbugs, ants, beetles, spiders, flies, fleas or anything else.

I informed her that I would immediately contact the State of NJ's Department of Community Affairs which I promptly did. I again attempted to reach Mr. Hawthorn at 3:56pm but he did not answer so I left a message. Andrea sent me an email stating that my late fee was now due immediately and that it was no longer $25 but $75.

Rule #4...No changes can be made to the lease until the current lease ends. Please be aware that a landlord can't just raise your rent because they feel like it. They have to wait until the termination of your current lease to do so.

In most states in America it is illegal for a landlord to retaliate against a tenant for exercising a legal right such as complaining to a government agency. In New Jersey, it is illegal for a landlord to raise the rent after a tenant has complained to a government agency.

As noted on the legal website NOLO, **New Jersey state law (N.J. Stat. Ann. §§ 2A:42-10.10, 2A:42-10.12 2) prohibits landlords from retaliating against tenants.**

"Tenant Rights Protected Against Landlord Retaliation in New Jersey

It is illegal for a landlord to retaliate against a tenant in New Jersey who has exercised a legal right, including:

- *complaining to the landlord about unsafe or illegal living conditions*

- *complaining to a government agency, such as a building or health inspector, about unsafe or illegal living conditions*

- *assembling and presenting your views collectively — for example, by joining or organizing a tenant union, or*

- *exercising a legal right allowed by your state or local law, such as withholding the rent for an uninhabitable unit.*

Types of Retaliation That Are Against State Law

The kinds of retaliatory acts covered by New Jersey law include terminating a tenancy or filing an eviction lawsuit; increasing the rent; or decreasing services, such as locking the laundry room."

It is assumed to be retaliation if the rent increase is implemented within so many months of a protected act. My increase came within hours of complaining to the Borough. (According to my lease, late fees are included as rent).

I informed Co-Owner Jonathan Stein of the above events. I also sent him pictures of me stuffing a 341 page book into the hole in the bedroom floor to illustrate how big it is.

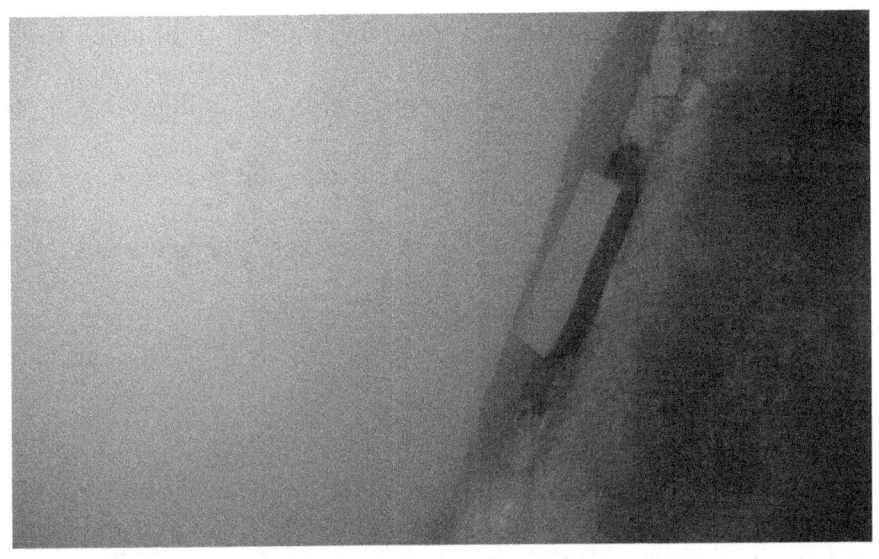

I also made a video showing me dropping a large roll of tape, white out, and a cell phone through the hole and it all landing outside on the ground. These things were done because no matter how well you're able to describe something pictures and videos always do a better job of relaying your message.

Sure enough, on August 9th an Inspector/Pest Control Technician from Erlich came and conducted an inspection, which I videotaped, and found nothing. He came wearing latex gloves and inspected beds, mattresses, bedding, pillows, sofas. You name it and he searched it. I asked to receive a copy of the report. He stated that because Summit paid for it only they could get a copy.

A few days later I got a call back from one of the producers of Jim Donovan's 3 On Your Side in response to my email detailing my situation. I sent a copy of the message to Summit Place's Co-Owner. Two hours later the repairs were made, but, only after the intervention of Channel 3 News.

A few days later, Summit had maintenance remove a large portion of the kitchen cabinets from my apartments. They said that they were going to "fix" the cabinets because the doors were crooked/loose.

They did not return them until Monday, August 18, 2014. The doors were fixed. Really?! Who in their right mind honestly believes that kitchen cabinets need to be taken down from the wall, sent out and then brought back days later to have them tightened?! Surely screws could have been tightened right there on the spot. Yes, I was just as amazed as you are. I believe (this is my opinion) they were trying to find some evidence of a bug infestation that does not exist to corroborate the false allegation that I had complained of bedbugs.

Days later, I went to the Clerk's Office at Superior Court of NJ and got a copy of the Certification of Breach of Consent Judgment that Andrea McDonald had signed. The Breach said that on June 20, 2014, in the presence of Summit Place Attorney, Andrew Sklar, Andrea had falsely reported that I had breached the consent judgment by not paying $801 as agreed upon on or before 6/12/14 which, of course, was totally false.

Andrew Sklar, Esquire
Sklar Law, LLC
1200 Laurel Oak Rd. Ste 102
Voorhees, NJ 08043
856/258-4050
Attorneys for Plaintiff
File No.: LT227

DRA LINDENWOLD, LLC	SUPERIOR COURT OF NEW JERSEY
	CAMDEN COUNTY
Plaintiff(s)	LAW DIVISION - SPECIAL CIVIL PART
	DOCKET NO.: LT-3826-14
	CIVIL ACTION
Angela Harris	CERTIFICATION OF BREACH OF
	CONSENT JUDGMENT
Defendant(s)	

On June 12, 2014, the tenant in the above matter breached the consent judgment entered into between the landlord and tenant. The facts upon which the claim of breach is based is as follows:

Tenant was required to pay $801 on or before 6/13/14. Tenant did not make the payment.

Based on said breach, I request that the warrant of removal be issued and/or executed in accordance with the provisions of the law. I hereby certify that the foregoing statements by me are true. I am aware that if any of the foregoing statements made by me are false I am subject to punishment.

_____   _____
                                   Angela L. McDonald, Property Manager

A copy of this certification was mailed by regular mail to the tenant on: 6/20/14
A copy of this certification was served on the door of the premises on: _____

                                   _____
                                   Andrew Sklar

This is a picture of the money orders that I used to pay along with the dates that money orders had been cashed, as well as the phone number to call to verify this information. (*The money orders were still blank in this picture but it is easily verifiable when they were cashed by simply calling the customer service number shown on the money orders*).

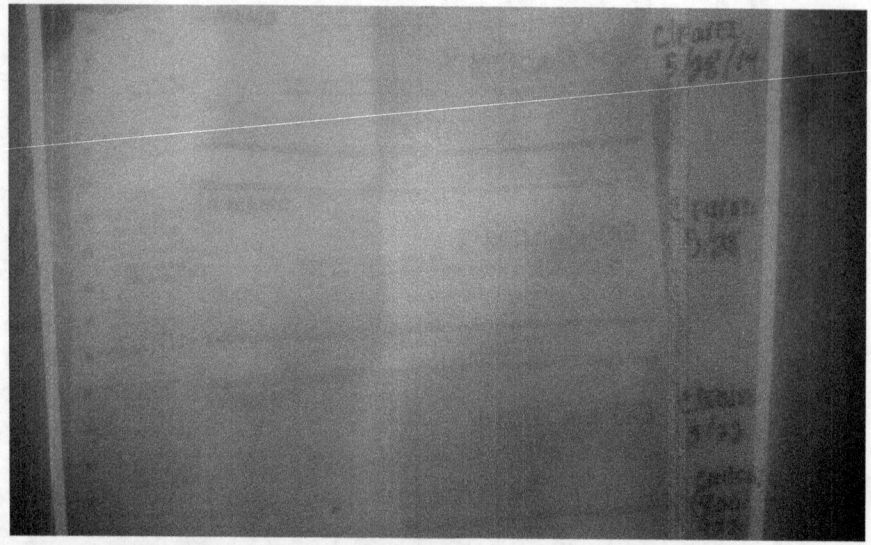

This sworn statement also contradicts paperwork from Emergency Assistance,

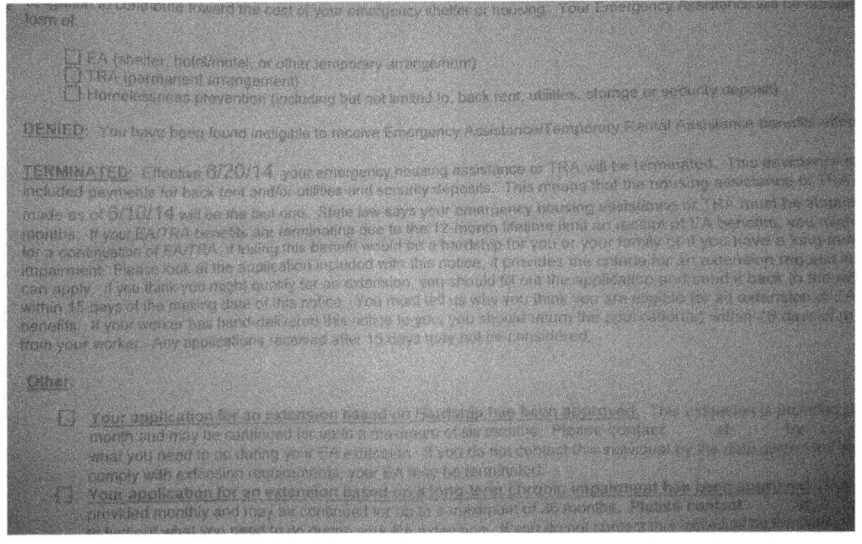

Of course this same paperwork is in the possession of both myself and EA. Also, Andrea falsely stated that I had received a copy of the certification. I never received a copy, not by regular mail, certified or tacked to my front door. Lying on a sworn certification constitutes perjury under federal law: 18 U.S.C. 1621. It is also a crime under New Jersey law; NJSA 2C:28-1.

The false reports and fuzzy math seemed unending. After accepting my rental payment for September. Leasing Agent, Makini Corsey then gave me a paper stating that I owed $150 in late fees. I informed Makini that I was now recording our interaction *(so of course this entire exchange is on video)*. I then aimed the video recorder down so that she would not be on video, only her explanation of the late fees. She said that she doesn't give her permission. I told her that NJ is a One Party Consent state (meaning that New Jersey is a state in which only one party to the conversation needs to give consent to being recorded…so if the person doing the recording gives consent, then that's all that is needed) and that I didn't need her permission and that I was being nice by informing her. She insisted that NJ is a two-party consent state. Finally, I asked for a copy of my account transactions. She refused.

The following day there was a notice placed on the door of Summit's Office stating that Summit does not allow the use of audio or video recording devices in the offices. It further stated

that the use of such devices are prohibited on the premises.

PLEASE BE ADVISED THAT
SUMMIT PLACE DOES NOT
ALLOW THE USE OF AUDIO
OR VIDEO RECORDING
DEVICES IN THE OFFICE.

THE USE OF SUCH
DEVICES ARE PROHIBITED
ON THE PREMISES.

THANK YOU FOR YOUR COOPERATION.
MANAGEMENT

The following lists some of the more common issues encountered by New Jersey renters. This list is by no means exhaustive.

Rule #5…Keep All Receipts

Without abiding by this first rule, you are almost guaranteed to be on the losing side of any legal battle. Had I not had my receipts I would not have been granted a Show Cause Hearing to challenge my complex' attempted illegal eviction. In fact, language is built right into the forms that you use asking if you have proof of having paid your rent. No matter how nice the landlord or property manager may be, still insist on getting a receipt.

Rule #6…Get Everything In Writing

There is no substitute for having agreements in writing. If you don't get everything in writing, as far as the judge is concerned it's just "he said, she said" and "your word against his." Sometimes people feel uncomfortable asking for something in writing because it may seem to imply that you don't trust the other party. I can tell you that you will be much more uncomfortable in court after the judge rules against you because you didn't get it in writing.

Rule#7...Document Everything Then Keep The Documentation

In social work there is a very popular saying, "if it isn't documented it didn't happen." The young couple mentioned earlier had documentation on hand when the landlord tried to illegally evict them by having the sheriff accompany him as he changed the locks. They were able to show receipts where they had paid the landlord after making payment arrangements and that the Warrant of Removal had expired months previously. In New Jersey the Warrant expires after 30 days if not executed unless the landlord notifies the tenant and petitions the court.

http://www.judiciary.state.nj.us/rules/r6-7.htm

N.J.S.A. 2A:42-10.17 *A warrant of removal shall not be executed earlier than the third business day after service on a residential tenant. If a judgment for possession is entered in a summary action for the recovery of premises and the landlord fails to apply in writing for a warrant of removal within 30 days after the entry of the judgment, or if the warrant is not executed within 30 days of its issuance, such warrant shall not thereafter be issued or executed, as the case may be, except on application to the court and written notice to the tenant served at least seven days prior thereto by simultaneously mailing same by both certified and ordinary mail or in the manner prescribed for service of process in landlord/tenant actions by R. 6:2-3(b); provided, however, that either 30 day period may be tolled for the duration of any order for orderly removal or any other court initiated stay, extended by court order or written agreement executed by the parties subsequent to the entry of the judgment and filed with the clerk. For purposes of this rule, entry of judgment shall be defined as the date upon which the right to request a warrant for removal.*

Rule #8…You Have A Right To Clean and Safe Housing

All tenants have a right to clean and safe housing. There is a reasonable expectation that the landlord will keep the unit in a habitable condition. New Jersey Department of Community Affairs, more commonly referred to as DCA, is responsible for setting the codes and standards of apartments in the state. DCA states, "Habitability Tenants have the right to safe, sanitary and decent housing. Residential leases carry an "implied warranty of habitability." This means that a landlord has a duty to maintain the rental unit and keep it fit for residential purposes throughout the entire term of the lease and that the landlord must repair damage to vital facilities. The tenant is responsible for maintaining and returning the property to the landlord in the same condition that the tenant received it, except for normal wear.

Note: Where damage has been caused by malicious or abnormal use by the tenant, the tenant is responsible for the repair.

Mold

I absolutely must address the issue of mold. Mold , certain types of black mold in particular, is a very serious health threat and should be reported to management immediately. My family and I have been victims of mold toxicity. The entire ordeal was a nightmare that I wouldn't wish on my worst enemy.

I informed maintenance that there was mold along the bottom of my bedroom wall as well as the along the same adjoining wall in my kids' room. The maintenance man, Cephas, then asked me if I had heard the sump pump lately. Prior to Cephas informing me months earlier that there was one under my bedroom floor, I had never heard of a sump pump. I told him that I hadn't heard it in a while and that I couldn't tell him when the last time was that I heard it. At this point, I still don't know what a sump pump is, what it looks like or what it's used for.

After talking to management, Cephas did wipe the wall with a bleach solution. I asked him to please have it done professionally because a mere bleach solution was not enough. He assured me that more intense treatment would follow and that I would receive two follow up letters from management.

Well, he was right. A couple of days later I received two letters from Summit's attorney, Andrew Sklar. (I know what you're thinking and I agree… to my knowledge most cease and desist letters come from property managers and not their attorney). They were cease and desist orders. One order stated that I had bothered a neighbor's guest by banging on the walls and the other letter stated that I had been late repeatedly and if I was late once more I'd be evicted. However, there was no letter regarding the mold or further treatment to remove it.

I did receive an email from Andrea that read:

Good Afternoon Angela,

This is in response to your email I received on Monday 1/12/15. Please be advised that DRA Lindenwold has satisfactorily corrected and repaired discoloration in both bedrooms as requested on your maintenance work order number 000004 dated 1/2/15. No further action will be taken.

Please be aware that there are no sump pumps on the premises. (Emphasis added are mine)

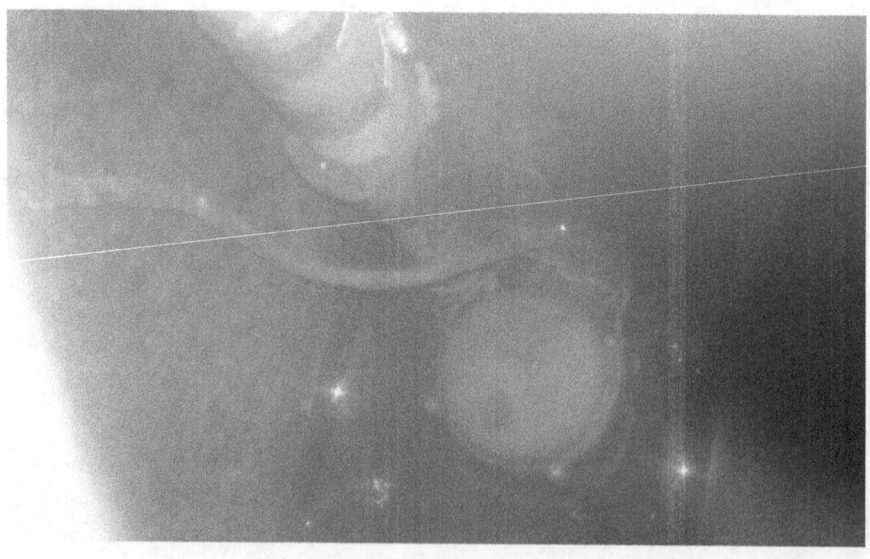

This is the non-existent sump pump that is on the premises.

The preceding link is to the non-existing sump pump. As Summit dragged their feet in removing the mold properly, they refused to even acknowledge it as mold as my family and I got sicker and sicker. We ended up having all four of us sleep piled up in our living room to avoid any more exposure from the mold in the bedroom.

If you're anything like I was you have no idea what a sump pump is for. It's installed in homes that are prone to flooding. It's the sump pumps job to collect the water that is pooling and shoot it aware from the residence. Most experts agree sump pumps should not be in bedrooms. If they malfunction dirty, black, stagnant, moldy water will just be sitting under your floor spreading further and further.

To make matters worse, the sump pump had been inaccessible for some time as the wooden covering to it was nailed shut.

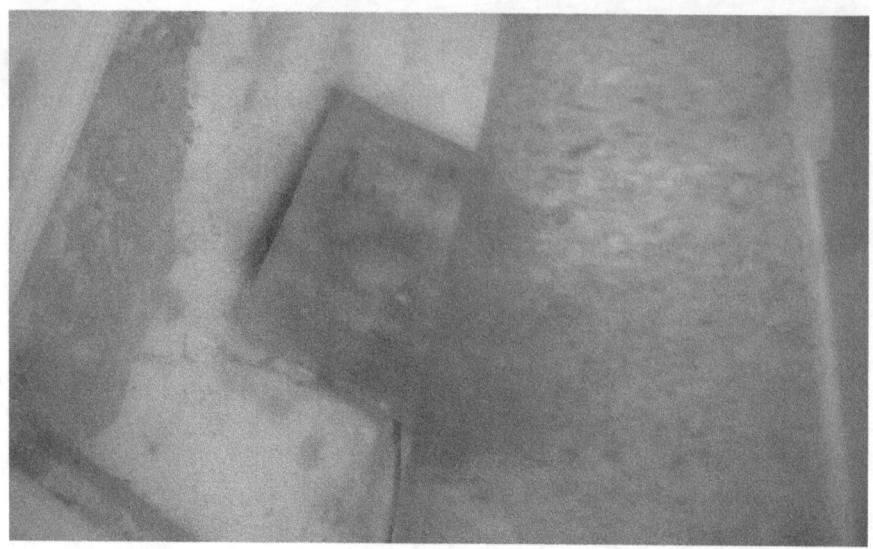

This is the moldy carpet and board covering the sump pump.

I kept wondering why staff would never come and open it so we could see exactly what we were dealing with. I discovered it open quite by accident. I had brought someone over so they could see the covering that I had been talking so much about, there was an electrical cord running from the sump pump to the bedroom wall and through the hole in the wall to outside. I had even sent an email to Lindenwold Inspections stating as much,

---

Subject: RE: Mold

Good afternoon.

My name is Angela Davis. I reside at Summit Place Apts #509. I am writing to inquire as to what is proper mold clean up and to request that the complex repair the source of the mold problem. The area outside of my back bedrooms stays saturated with water even days after it rains. I was initially told by Summit that there was a sump pump under my bedroom floor, then I was told that there was no sump pump there. Well, there is something under my bedroom floor because there is an electrical cord that runs from under the floorboard and under the wall leading to outside. My complex cleaned the mold once, only to have it come back a few days later and also show up in new locations as well. This leads me to believe there is more mold is present although not visible because the source of the standing water problem has not been addressed. Also, there is a disgusting orange ball at the base of the wall outside of my bedroom that may or may not be related to the mold problem. It looks like some type of fungus or other growth (of course I'm not sure because this is not my area of expertise). In closing, if anything further can be done to get to the source of the water/ mold problem I a requesting that it be done.

Thanks
Angela Davis

On this particular day the covering had been removed and placed to the side but my moldy carpet had been placed back over top of it. I went to Andrea and demanded to know why someone had entered my unit when I was not home. She denied that anyone had been there. I'm certain that the covering to the sump pump did not unbolt itself. I sent them an email reminding that under no circumstances were they to be in my apartment without permission. When I saw how disgusting and mold covered the sump pump, the water and the cover was I began to understand why no one had ever come into my apartment and opened the sump pump cover in front of me. After all, how could they...according to them there were no sump pumps on the premises.

As if my family and I hadn't gone through enough with Summit, the same Lindenwold Inspector who falsely stated that **I said** I had bedbugs, took a week to get back to me about this current mold problem. Due to his lack of honesty during our last interaction, this time I sent him an email and CC'd it to a member of City Council. This is how my email reads:

further can be done to get to the source of the water/ mold problem I

a requesting that it be done.

I didn't get a response until 7 days later. He left a voicemail message stating that he inspected the outside of the unit and there were several violations given to Summit. I called and requested a copy of his report on February 9th. I even went in person and requested a copy of the report and the woman at the counter wrote down my information and said she would give him the message.

Eventually, he did cite the complex for numerous violations but they were given an open-ended date in which to make the repairs. Meanwhile, I had to hire a private contractor to test my home and he found it to be at twice the normal level for a certain type of black mold.

Rule #9... Even before you move into your apartment there should be a Certificate of Occupancy which lets you know that the unit was inspected and deemed to be safe and ready to be occupied by a tenant. Always do your own inspection of the unit and make a list of needed repairs. Both you and the landlord should sign it and date it. Signing and dating all important agreements and documentation is extremely important because it shows that you gave the landlord enough time to make repairs or to address whatever situation is of concern.

Lease Agreements

Make sure to get a copy of your lease agreement with both you and the landlord's signature and date. A lease can be either verbal or written and is a contract between you and the landlord. The lease is extremely important and can greatly impact the quality of your residency so be sure to read it very carefully. If you ever go to court, get a lawyer, or seek help from a social service agency like South Jersey Legal Services, they will always, always refer back to your lease. **Rule #10...The terms of the lease are not enforceable if it violates New Jersey laws or statutes, other than that, what the lease says is what it is.**

Just because your lease ends does not mean that you have to move out. If your landlord wants you out, he still has to go through the eviction process. The law is very clear about this.

This is true even if a person was allowed to stay in an apartment as a part of his employment. In my old complex, the maintenance person was fired. He was subsequently given two weeks to remove his belongings and get out. This was done without a court order or even an eviction notice. It should have been up to the courts to order the maintenance person to vacate.

The person was about to leave simply because the management office told him to but they locked him out before he even had a chance to move all of his belongings. In New Jersey, this is considered a misdemeanor and he should have immediately called police to gain entrance into his apartment.

He was the victim of a self-help eviction. This is when a landlord evicts a tenant without going through the courts and obtaining an order. It doesn't matter how badly a landlord wants a person out or how badly a tenant messes up, there still has to be a court ordered eviction for it to be legal. This is the case in most states.

Rent

As stated earlier, you should always get a receipt when you pay your rent no matter how you pay. The receipt should have the landlord's signature as well as the date. I had one unscrupulous property manager tell me that he wasn't allowed to give receipts and that he had just been told so during a meeting at Corporate. Even though it didn't sound right, at the time, I just did not have enough knowledge about my rights to challenge it. Today if I were to encounter a situation like that I would ask for him to please put it in writing. I would also send a follow-up email restating our entire conversation. In the email I would again request a receipt. At the end of the email I'd make a notation stating, "Also sent via certified mail." Then I'd print it out and send it via certified mail keeping a copy for myself along with a return receipt for proof that he actually received it.

Late Payments/Fees

Landlords can charge a late fee if the rent is not paid by an agreed upon date, usually the 1st of the month. In New Jersey tenants have until the 5th calendar day. There are special circumstances in which tenants have until the 5th business day of the month to pay the rent before a late fee is assessed. This statute is for tenants who receive Social Security Old Age Pension, Welfare or Work First NJ, Social Security Income, Social Security Disability. *Cite:*

N.J.S.A. 2A: 42-6.1 and 6.3

The law states that a landlord must allow a tenant a period of "five business grace days" to pay the rent. If a tenant pays the rent in the five-day period, the landlord may not charge a late fee. In counting the five business days, do not include Saturday.

There are many landlords who are knowingly violating this statute. While I was president of our tenant's association, I repeatedly brought it to the attention of management that tenants who were covered under this statute was being charged late fees on the 5th calendar day and not business day. They absolutely would not budge. I ended up filing an injunction requesting that management to comply with this statute. In my complaint, I explicitly stated that I was not looking for any monetary compensation, I simply wanted Summit Apartments to cease and desist in assessing these illegal fees, Docket C106-14. **Rule #11... It's important to mention that filing motions and other legal paperwork can be really expensive. If, however, you can't afford to pay the fees you can file a waiver requesting that the fees be waived.** You must provide documentation of income to the court. Had I not filed for a fee waiver, it would have cost me $350 in total to file this injunction. I should also mention that I was representing myself in this case, also known as Pro Se.

The injunction hearing was held in January. The judge refused to allow me to file on behalf of all of the affected tenants. When I told her that the complex was being investigated by the Camden County Prosecutor's Office, after having been referred to the District Attorney's Office, she seemed to me to become even more irate and said, "so what! They haven't been indicted, there are no charges!" I told her that the investigation just began in December. She then demanded to know what for. I told her that when some tenants have paid money for their rent the money would just "disappear" and not be credited to their account. She waved her hand at me and said, "oh, that's just a billing era!" To my knowledge, she had never read any of the documentation nor heard from any of the victims. Then she told me that tenants didn't need to have until the date stated in the NJ statute they needed to pay by the 1st or else. She said that she knows that's what Landlord Tenant court does and that the Anti-Eviction Act is trying to avoid causing people to be homeless but she doesn't agree. As incredible as it may sound, every word of this is true. I invite you to read the transcripts for yourself. This is the reason that I have provided the docket number.

Still, everyone acknowledged that tenants who met the criteria were covered under the statute and therefore actually did have until the 5th business day to pay their rent before being considered late, to the best of my knowledge, however, the complex still has not changed their policy to reflect this.

Landlord Entering Premises

As a tenant, when you rent your home, there is a reasonable expectation of you being able to have quiet enjoyment. You have a right to not have your landlord or property manager just enter your home at will. They certainly do have a right, however, to enter your home without your permission if there is an emergency. Your landlord should make arrangements with you to do inspections, make repairs, show the unit to prospective buyers and/or tenants. Some unethical landlords attempt to harass tenants by repeatedly coming to their unit. If you or someone you know is experiencing this you should immediately send a certified letter requesting that the behavior stop. If it doesn't, keep detailed documentation of dates, times, reasons for the intrusion and be prepared to go to court if necessary.

I sincerely hope that my experiences are helpful to you. This is an abridged, much shorter version of my book as I thought it best to get it out as soon as possible. Recently, my family and I have experienced ongoing cyber attacks. My emails, Facebook and several files have been accessed. I find myself having to quickly learn about Cyber Security. This book absolutely needed to be published.

www.ingramcontent.com/pod-product-compliance
Lightning Source LLC
Chambersburg PA
CBHW070942180526
45168CB00003B/1144